Don't Squat With Yer Spurs On!

II

Texas Bix Bender

Illustrations by L. Bark'karie

GIBBS·SMITH
P
PUBLISHER

SALT LAKE CITY

05 04 03 02   10 09 08 07

Text copyright © 1997 by Texas Bix Bender
illustrations copyright © 1997 by L. Berk'karie

Published by
Gibbs Smith Publisher
P.O. Box 667
Layton, Utah 84041

Cover design and art by L. Bark'karie
Interior design by Mary Ellen Thompson. TTA Design
Printed and bound in the U.S.A.

Library of Congress Cataloging-in-Publication Data

Bender, Texas Bix, 1949 –
        Don't squat with yer spurs on! II / by Texas Bix
        Bender, illustrated by L. Bark'karie – 1st ed.
        p. cm.

        ISBN 0-87905-832-3
        1. Cowboys–West(U.S.)–Humor.
        2. West (U.S.)–Social life and customs–Humor.
        3. Cowboys writings. American–West(U.S.)
        4. Bark'karie. L., ill. II. Title.
        F596.B325 1997
        978-dc21   97-6876
                                        CIP

Other funny little books by
Texas Bix Bender and Gladiola Montana:

Don't Squat With Yer Spurs On!

Never Ask a Man the
Size of His Spread

Just One Fool Thing After Another

Laughing Stock

A Cynic's Guide to Love

Hats and the Cowboys
Who Wear Them

Don't Throw in the Trowel

50 Good Reasons to Be
/ Not to Be a Cowboy

50 Good Reasons to
/ Not to Diet

7 Habits for Highly Happy People

To order, call toll free
(1-800) 748-5439

To my companions in the trail drive:
Too Slim, Woody Paul, Ranger Doug, Joey
the Cowpolka King, Professor Zeno Clinker,
Deputy Dave, Bert, Theresa, Diane, Patty,
Mayo, Lisa, Brandon, my sister Eileen, and
especially and always, Sal.

The Cowboy Code

In sun and shade,
be sure by your friends.
Never swing a mean loop.
Never do dirt
to man nor animal.

The good thing
about cowboying is
that any boss will gladly
give you eighteen hours
to do your day's work.

If you find you're drinking
most of your entertainment
out of a can, it's time to look
for your fun elsewhere.

A stranger's business
ain't yours.

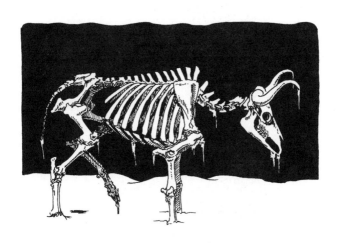

When cattle die
standing up,
it's hard times.

You wanta be careful
that a freshly branded calf
ain't suckin' at
the wrong cow.

Avoid flasharity, foofaraw,
and fumadiddle in dress,
speech, and conduct.
Leave the peacocking
for the peacocks.

There's no use for a man
who owns a dog
to do the barking himself.

We might not be so bad off
if we had a little less
of everything.

The best way to set
a record is to be a good
ways off from any
tape measures, scales,
or witnesses.

If your job is to shovel,
and all you can see
ahead is dirt,
it's time to change jobs.

Before you let anybody
measure you for
the big wooden overcoat,
make sure you've wrung
all the life out of your livin'.

A good pard will ride with
you till hell freezes over—
and a little while on the ice.

In the mounting of a horse,
the right side
is the wrong side,
and the left side
is the right side.
Your backside
is the broadside,
and that's the side
you sit on.

Some waddies
take a little time to
work it up and spit it out.
Give it to 'em.
Life ain't so short
that you can't take the time
to hear a man out.

A mixed herd of
both sexes and all ages
is the easiest kind
to manage.

You will find it is always easier
to walk if there is a horse
between your legs.

A Texas breakfast is
a two-pound hunk of steak,
a quart of whisky,
and a hound dog.
If you're wondering why
you need the dog—
well, somebody has
to eat the steak.

Given the right dose
of prickly pear,
any nag will buck.

When you're in the wrong
and you need to set it right,
how far you have traveled
in the doin' of it
has nothing to do
with the rightin' of it.

If you've got a voice
like a burro with a bad cold
— the kind that makes
a coyote cringe —
don't risk singin' to the herd.

A cowboy wears
his bandana for
the same reason
he wears his pants:
He ain't decent
without it.

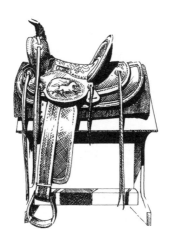

If you're gonna itch
to have somethin',
better be ready
to scratch for it.

You cannot improve
somebody's part by
combing their head
with a six-shooter.

Anytime you find
a little shade,
take it.

If you own it and run it and
have cattle on it — even if
you owe the moon on it —
it's yours and you're
a cattleman.
That's what folks'll call you.
They may call you
a good one or a bad one,
but they'll call you
a cattleman.

This ain't
the same ol' range.

If you lead somebody
around by the nose,
it don't say much for them.
It says even less for you.

When you get bucked off,
the easiest way to explain it
is to say you dropped your
hat and got off in
a hurry to get it.

Most bonanzas are
just holes in the ground
owned by big bullshitters.

It's the work, not the clock,
that tells you when
it's quittin' time.

If a cowboy drops by
around dinnertime,
it's okay to say,
"What the hell do you want?"
But you still have to
invite him in for dinner.

Building and fixing fences
wouldn't be so bad
if you didn't have to
get off your horse to do 'em.

You can't weigh the facts
if you've got the scales
loaded down
with your opinions.

See the heavens, smell the air,
taste the dust and the alkali, hear
the wind and the wild,
feel the motion of your horse. . . .
On a good day,
that's all you need.
On a bad day,
that's all you need.

If you want to liven up
a conversation,
just say the right thing
the wrong way.

Cattle guards are grates
in the road that keep cattle
from crossing. They are not
women with whistles and
stop signs who help
the cattle safely
cross the road.

A few sweet words
and a little bit of kindness
can coax the hottest iron
outta the fire.

When it's your butt
that's about to go flyin',
try to have more
common sense than pride.
Go ahead and choke
the horn and
claw the leather.

Don't make
a long story short
just so you can
tell another one.

It's hard to keep a secret
around the campfire
after a hearty meal of
pinto whistleberries.

When you forgive
and forget,
forget that you forgave
while you're at it.

If you're wonderin' what this ol' world is comin' to, you're in the same shoes as your daddy, your daddy's daddy, and every other daddy that's come down the trail.

If you're ridin' a high horse,
there ain't no way to get
down off it gracefully.

However one-sided
a man may be,
he will have other sides
if you look hard enough.

The best way to knock
a chip off a shoulder
is with a friendly pat
on the back.

A little mud on
the carpet from the boots
of honest, working cowboys
is a lot better than
a slick-soled bandbox
sitting in a parlor chair.

Work less at worrying and
more at working.

Advice is like a pot of chili:
You should try a little of it
yourself before you give
anybody else a taste.

A hand that ain't there
when you need it
is kinda like a blister —
only shows up
when the work's all done.

If you ain't pullin' your weight,
you're pushin' your luck.

Sorry looks back.
Worry looks around.
Faith looks up.

If the job you did
speaks for itself,
don't interrupt.

Doin' things the smart way
don't cost half as much
as doing 'em
the stupid way.

Nothin' keeps you honest
more than witnesses.

Sometimes courage
takes no more than
sittin' down, suckin' it in,
and listenin'.

There's a high cost
to low living.

You can always find
free cheese
in a mousetrap.

Cowboying would be
a lot more pleasant
if Noah had taken the time
to swat a couple of
mosquitoes on his ark.

Never be too quick
to criticize yourself.
It's not fair to all your
friends and relatives
who are dyin'
to do it for you.

A week spent
around a campfire
will tell you more about
a man than a decade
spent living next door
to him.

Just because some yahoo
puts Tabasco
in your oatmeal don't mean
you gotta eat it.

The purest metal
comes out of
the greatest heat.

Going faster when you're
lost won't help a bit.

Never bluff
when you're dealin' with
a woman.

If you're carryin' a big roll,
dress down,
not up.

If you have to count
your chickens before
they're hatched, keep it
to yourself. Nobody gives a
damn how many chickens
you're gonna have.

If you are careless
by nature, you have to learn
to be careful
as a necessity.

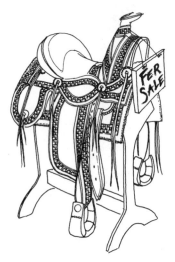

Soft grub, feather beds,
and easy livin'
can lead to a sold saddle.

You're not bein' diplomatic
just because you put
"please" in front of
"shut the hell up."

Sometimes it takes
a lot more thinkin'
to deal with changes
than to make 'em.

If you meet up with
an alligator and he's
as scared as you are,
the water won't be
fit to drink.

There are rules to
horse ridin', but the horse
won't necessarily
know them.

"Look out" usually means
"Don't look, duck!"

If somebody says
you ride like you're part
of the horse, you might
wanta ask 'em which part
they're talking about.

You generally learn
the value of money
from a lack of it.

There's no better friend
than a horse that's saddled
and ready to go.

It's easy to see things
you're lookin' for.
The trick is to see things
you're not lookin' for.

When a running horse
gets to the edge of a cliff,
it's way too late to say "whoa."

You'll feel better
when it quits hurtin'.

A horse ain't trying
to be polite
when he comes
to a fence and
lets you go over first.

The problem with money
is not so much
where it goes,
but how to get ahold of it
to start with.

It's better to have
a good horse for a year
than an ass
for all its life.

It's always a bit confusin'
when somethin' goes right.

Most anybody
can be a cowboy,
but it takes a damn genius
to make any money at it.

Entering the
Publishers' Clearinghouse
Sweepstakes every year
is not considered
a well-thought-out
retirement plan.

One good thing
about being a cowboy
is that you just don't
have time for golf.

Wrong no man and
write no woman.

The old saying that
familiarity breeds contempt
does not apply
to rattlesnakes.

Beware the pessimist—
the sorta hombre who
hangs around the train depot
and tells everybody the train
"is never gonna get here."
When it chugs into view, he says,
"They'll never get that thing
stopped." When it stops, he says,
"Uh huh, they'll never get it
started again." When it fires up
and heads off, he says,
"Well, that's the last
we'll ever see of that thing."

The softer the head,
the bigger the hat.

The bigger the mouth,
the better it looks shut.

When your head's
in the bear's mouth
is not the time to be
smacking him on the nose
and calling him names.

Eat with your fingers
only if the food
is clean.

How long you live
has nothin' to do with
how long you're dead.

There is no need
to fear water:
It makes a good chaser.

Nature gave us all somethin'
to fall back on,
and sooner or later
we all land flat on it.

You can't tell how
far a frog can jump
by his croak.

Watch about sayin'
"it can't be done."
Somebody's liable to
interrupt you by doin' it.

Hard-boiled eggs
are yellow at the core.

If there's a hole in your
story or your fence,
whatever you'd rather
didn't get out—will.

Believe in miracles,
but don't bet on 'em.

Enjoy being yourself . . .
whatever that is.

Just 'cause you're following
a well-marked trail
don't mean that
whoever made it
knew where they
were goin'.

Lonesome brings on
ailments that only
company can cure.

Always walk tall and keep
your head up —
unless you're walkin' in
a cow pasture.

A gate only works
if a corral comes with it.

Whether the glass is
half empty or half full
depends on whether
you're drinkin' or pourin'.

Never sit
a barbwire fence
naked.

Never go through a gate
without closing it
behind you.

Things have a way
of workin' out if you
just keep your head.

If your knees hurt too much,
your stirrups are too short.
If your tail end hurts too much,
your stirrups are too long.
If they both hurt,
your stirrups are just right.

Money may buy you a dog,
but only love
can make him wag his tail.

There is never a shortage
of good horse sense
on this planet. Of course,
it's mostly the horses
that have it.

If horses and dogs
aren't in heaven,
I'd just as soon
go to Texas.

The quickest way to
feel rich is to figure out
what you can do without.

Never believe anybody
who says their horse
doesn't kick.

If at first you don't succeed,
try to hide
your astonishment.

There are a lot of reasons
to love a horse.
Sometimes it's no more
than the sweet little way
he stepped on some
big ass's foot.

The best way
to break a bad habit
is to drop it.

When arguin' with a woman,
always remember this
little phrase,
"Maybe you're right."

"We come into this world
all naked and bare,
We go out of this world
we know not where.
But if we have been good
cowboys here,
We need not fear what's
waitin' for us there."

— *Favorite toast of*
Ab Blocker,
legendary trail driver